Soulful Verses

Pratibha Payyadi

BookLeaf
Publishing

India | USA | UK

Presentation by *BookLeaf Publishing*

Web: www.bookleafpub.com

E-mail: info@bookleafpub.com

ISBN: 9789363319899

First edition 2024

*This book is dedicated to the ones who inspire
me to feel deeply and embrace the full spectrum
of human emotion.*

*To my revered Guru [Sadhguru], your presence
in my life has been a blessing beyond measure.
I am forever grateful for the grace bestowed
upon me.*

*To my parents, Nirmala and Suryaprakash,
whose unwavering love, support and
encouragement have been the guiding light of
my journey through life. Your zest for life
inspires me to try new things!*

*To my spouse Udoay, who is my bouncing
board. Your belief in me has given me the
courage to pursue my dreams and express
myself through poetry.*

*To my cherished daughter Navani and my
beloved son-in-law Pradeep, your immense and
boundless love fill my heart with joy and
gratitude everyday. You are the anchor that
keeps me steady.*

My dear brother Aadarsh and his lovely wife Dipti. Your friendship, laughter and support have enriched my life in countless ways.

It is only fair that I dedicate my work to the little ones Vivaan, Shivaansh and Moksh; you are my greatest inspiration and immeasurable source of happiness, and joy.

To my dear friends Basavaraj, Sonali, Dr Sudhir Baldota for having my back. You are just amazing.

To Leo, who brought joy, companionship and unconditional love into my life. Though you may no longer be with us, your memory lives on forever in my heart and your presence deeply in my soul.

To all of you and countless other well-wishers not mentioned here, you have shaped my journey with your love, guidance and support; this book is a tribute to the profound impact you have had on my life . May these poems serve as a reflection of the beauty and complexity of human experience and may they resonate with

*you in moments of joy , sorrow and everything
in between.*

With deepest gratitude and love

Pratibha

ACKNOWLEDGEMENT

I would like to express my heartfelt gratitude to all those who have supported and inspired me on this journey of writing *Soulful Verses.*

First and foremost, I am deeply thankful to my family and friends for their unwavering encouragement and belief in my creative endeavours. Your love and support have been my greatest source of strength and inspiration.

I am also grateful to the countless poets and writers whose work has shaped and enriched my understanding of poetry. Your words have sparked my imagination and guided my own artistic journey.

I extend my heartfelt appreciation to BookLeaf Publishing, whose dedication and expertise have been instrumental in bringing *Soulful Verses* to fruition. Your commitment to quality and passion for literature has made this collaboration a rewarding and enriching experience.

Last but not the least, I extend my gratitude to the readers who have embraced my poetry with open heart and mind. Your feedback and encouragement are a constant source of motivation and validation.

To each and everyone of you, I am grateful for being a part of this journey. Your presence and support mean the world to me.

With deepest gratitude
Pratibha Payyadi

PREFACE

Welcome to *Soulful Verses*. These poems are fragments of my journey, whispers from the heart gathered over time. They dance with joy, grapple with sorrow, and explore the quiet beauty of everyday moments. Within these pages, I hope you find moments of solace, inspiration and reflection when you journey through the pages.

Thank you for allowing me to share my heart with you through poetry. May *Soulful Verses* resonate within your heart and inspire moments of introspection and reflection.

Warm regards
Pratibha Payyadi

CONTENTS

New beginnings - Dawn of renewal

It is in quiet moments, that ink finds flow,
A life reborn, skill begins to show.
New chapters, the pen's delight,
Weaving fresh dreams in the morning light.

The past a guide, not a chain,
Old paths put aside, never in vain.
The melody of doubt plays it's tune,
A beginner's heart never immune.

Blank pages call out for something new,
With every dawn and dusk, a clearer view.
Of words yet to form, thoughts yet to tame,
Emotions too deep, without a name.

Every stumble, a lesson it brings,
And in the mistakes, wisdom rings.
Beneath the weight of bygone years,
We shed our doubts and silent fears.

Let's rise and greet the morning sun,
A journey new has just begun.
Fear not the journey, though it looks rough,
For in every beginning, the passage is tough.

Embrace the unknown with courage and grace,
And let the story unfold, at its own pace.

Resurgence through Grace

Spiralling down the abyss
I was -
A broken, shattered life.
No will to breathe nor to live
But to just rot and die.

Lo and behold- A Miracle!

The abyss is now your lap:
Where I find eternal bliss.
A new ME and a new birth!
A gift from thee!
I cannot define a Guru
But I know-
you are the one for me.

Enhancing every moment of my life
with immense Grace and compassion…
If not for you
this one would have been long gone,
that is absolutely true.

In moments of doubt
You have been my firm ground.
In confusion

Your profound wisdom I have found.

Thanking you with verses seems too minuscule,
And making myself an offering sounds too
pretentious.
So then,
For leading me closer to life's truths,
and holding my being in gentle embrace,
I bow down in reverence forever in your Grace.

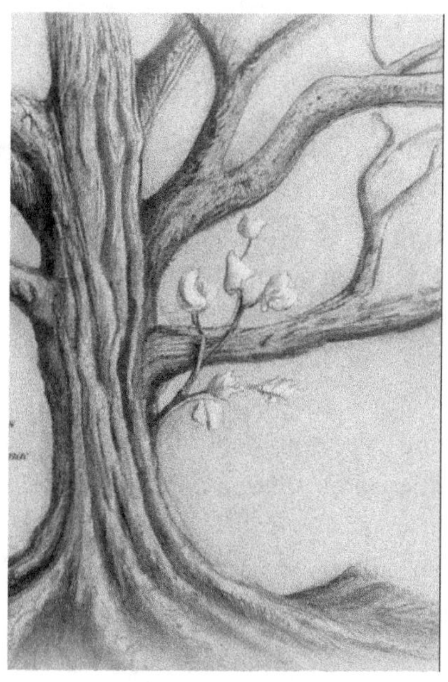

Fading paw prints

A soft, slow and steady entry
into our homes and hearts.
The depth of unconditional love,
deepening every moment,
creeping into your being part by part.

Entertainers they are,
of the very first grade.
They have you wound up around their paw-
mind you, there is no trade.
Seeking attention with their puppy eye and little
tugs.
What they bring to you - pure bliss and hugs.

And a day comes,
When the house is engulfed in silence...
There is no one to greet you at the door,
Nor anyone to overwhelm you with just a little
wag.

The little one, the baby of the house,
Has made the journey across the rainbow
bridge...
The great companion, loyal and true,
Has left deep paw prints all over you.

There - an empty space where he lay...
Pain in the heart just doesn't go away.

An Encounter with Death

A knock...
a reminder?
A visitor? A guest perhaps?
Have you come -
to walk a few steps in tandem?
Or,
Are you here to remind me of
my mortality?
Either way -
You are welcome!
For one, I shall enjoy your company
and accept you as you are.
And,
promise to gracefully tread the path, like a star!

The strength to carry out the promise,
Comes not from me;
but, from the one within
who is as vast as the sea.

So stay if you must or take me away.
I have been under the stars too long,
Trying to find my way.

Child's Embrace

As I held you in my arms
A promise I made…
To live every moment of my life joyfully with
you…
The promise looked easy at the outset
We have had our share of
Sunrise and Sunset.

We have grown together
Empowered each other…
You have helped me see life through your wide
eyes
Or should I say wise eyes?

We have fought tooth and nail in disagreement
We went hammer and tongs in argument.
We have giggled, chuckled and laughed together,

We have cried in pain and held on to each other.

The animated discussions we have had,
and continue having,
whether it is night or in the morning.

In every dialogue, individual perspective intact;
Through each exchange our voices interact.

And subject? No taboo.
Every thought embraced, open minds pursue.

Our journey of love
through laughter and tears,
Has been guided by hope
and we have conquered fears.

In your eyes I find the greatest reward
A bond unspoken, deeply adored, that is the real
award.

Thank you dearest for choosing our home,
In your warmth and love we never feel alone.
In you I see Love's pure art,
A masterpiece of Grace embedded deep in my
heart.

Celestial Symphony

The dramatic show
of celestial objects,
Illuminating the sky
with stunning effects.

Awaiting to rise as the
Sun vanishes below the horizon,
The stars emerging bright,
the magical night sky arising.

Galaxies spin in a distant dance
Leaving one mesmerised
And in a trance.

The night sky whispers without a word,
In the stillness,
Nothing is heard.
Of dreams and wishes and
Hopes set high, in the embrace of the night sky.

The silence humming songs that are old
Many mysteries yet to unfold.
Under the dome
of seemingly endless night,
We find our place and our sense of light.

Dreaming beneath this vast span,
One marvels at the cosmic plan.
In the night's tranquil hue,
We see the infinite, that is true!

The Bridge of Empathy

In a world so vast, yet most often cold,
Compassion is the warmth, that needs to unfold.

It is a gentle touch, a listening ear.
A light that is bright
when the skies are not clear.

It is also the eye that sees another's plight,
and then becomes the guiding light.
An extended hand, soft and kind
in unity, is it the rope that binds?

When words are few but actions speak,
Strength is found even when one is weak.
In times of grief, and in pain,
It is compassion that heals us again.

It is in compassion, we understand
the helping of a stranger's hand.
Knowing we are all the same,
Every heart beats in a fragile frame.

Flutters and Blooms

Shades of pink and hues of blue,
Flowers and petals, fresh and true.

Intoxicating fragrance fills the air,
As flowers bloom,
And butterflies in beautiful tints and shades,
flutter without a care.

They dance in Sun's warm embrace.
Their delicate wings flit with grace.
As colourful as they come,
A garden in full bloom is their home.

Each bloom narrates a story,
Each butterfly sings a song.
In this symphony of glory,
Is that where they belong!

Is each petal a canvas?
Each hue a tale?
Each butterfly a tiny albatross?
Hovering over flower,
leaving behind a trail?

In the magical embrace of nature's powers
We witness the beauty of butterflies and flowers.
In the garden where flows the gentle breeze,
We find our space and eternal peace.

Uncaged wings

In open skies and boundless plains,
Freedom's song a wild refrain.
With wings unfurled we soar on high,
In endless blue beneath the sky.

A song unsung, a spirit untamed,
A yearning deep, a freedom unnamed.
Not just on the lands where tyrants hold sway.
But in the heart, where shadows may play.

No chains to bind, no walls to cage,
Freedom's spirit knows no age.
To break the chain of doubt and despair,
To breathe the air without a care.

In every step in every stride,
It calls us forth, our fears to ride.
To dance with dreams, beneath open skies,
With laughter, light and fire in our eyes.

To speak our minds, though voice may shake,
For the right to choose and for justice's sake.
To dare to dream and reach the stars.
Freedom's light breaks through the bars.

Let us cherish, let us defend,
The precious gift freedom lends.
In its embrace we find our worth
A light that is bright on this temporary berth.

Let us fly with uncaged wings,
Embrace the dawn the future brings.
Freedom's song knows no bond,
A melody on hope's sacred ground.

Call of Kailash

Pristine peaks pierce the endless blue,
A canvas splashed in hues no mortal knew.
The Creator's brushstroke, a masterpiece bold,
Where colours dance and a story to unfold.

My journey, a Yatra, a scared quest,
A pilgrim's heart beats hard within my breast.
To Kailash, my Guru's abode - I tread,
Seeking oneness,
where the spirit dissolves but the body is unshed.

In my Master's gentle hold,
Each step a vow, a reverence untold.
Aware of his presence, a perch of trust,
I rode his shoulder, nonchalant dust.

Tears of ecstasy, unknown before,
well up in my eyes, brimming evermore.
To give without asking, that is his gentle art,
A silent language that warms my loyal heart.

Unaware of the sweetness to come,
I set out with an empty tongue.
A little taste, an intoxication, a nectar so bright,
Filled me with joy, and pure delight.
An intoxication, a blissful cascade,
Through every fibre, forever pervades.
Blessed is too weak, a simple word's claim,
This feeling inside, it is not the same.

This tangled self, a weight I cannot bear.
Yearning to shed it, dissolve in thin air.
Lost in the maze, no map to guide the way,
I yield to your hand, for you know how to play.

I am a fool perhaps, I relinquish control,
In your embrace, a calmness takes hold.
Let fragments fall, let pieces drift away,
Reborn anew, come what may.

Unpolished, flawed a canvas barely sketched
I stand before you, a sculpt scarcely etched
But in your gaze, a promise takes root,
A transformation, a blossoming fruit.

Gratitude's whisper pales in your light,
A meagre echo, a starless night.
You hold the vastness, the wisdom untold,
And see within me a story yet to unfold.

Golden cage

In smooth chains, a beauty held for hire,
A gilded cage...
Where innocence expires,
her eyes once bright, now hold a jaded gleam,
Reflecting desires, Not a joyful dream.

A stranger's cold embrace,
A loveless dance, a fake smile upon her face.
Words spoken - sweet promises untrue,
A body bartered, what else is there to do?

The scent of jasmine masks a hidden tear,
Laughter with a hollow echoing fear.
Silks and jewels, a facade so grand,
Too many scars on a harem land.

She is called a flower, a delicate bloom,
Despite the distress in her room.
For all the hungry eyes, she is just a fleeting
prize,
A pleasure bought, lust in the eyes.

But under layers, a spirit still remains,
A yearning for freedom, escaping the chains.
To chase a dream, beneath a starlit sky,
Where love's embrace wouldn't make her cry.

Will dawn ever smile on her endless night?
Will a gentle hand set her spirits alight?
Or is she destined to always roam,
A lost fragile bird, with nowhere to call home.

Song of devotion

No grand gestures or loud displays,
Your love so quiet in a thousand ways.

A hand to hold when shadows creep.
A listening ear and compassion deep.

A look that says - I understand
A silent vow, a helping hand.

Devotion whispers a soft song true,
For every action for me from you.

A bond that grows year by year
A love so deep dispelling fear.

In whispers soft, your praise I sing,
My life on a platter to you I bring.

With a grateful heart my devotion flows,
A blooming flower - inner fragrance grows.

Open palms

Not wealth, but a gift of soul,
Open palms, make others whole.
A listening ear, a kind embrace,
A blessing in life's rat race.

A quiet smile with a thoughtful deed,
Planting a tree, the shade others may need.
Time freely given without a thought spared,
A gentle word and a burden shared.

Generosity is a warmth that flows,
From a heart where kindness grows.
Nothing asked, no price to pay,
Deep love that lights another's way.

Open palms and hearts,
Help in easing life's smarts.
In this giving,
Lies true receiving.

From hands that give with pure intent,
Springs joy that knows content.
A heart unselfish, open and wide,
Brings joy to all on the ride.

Duality of Life

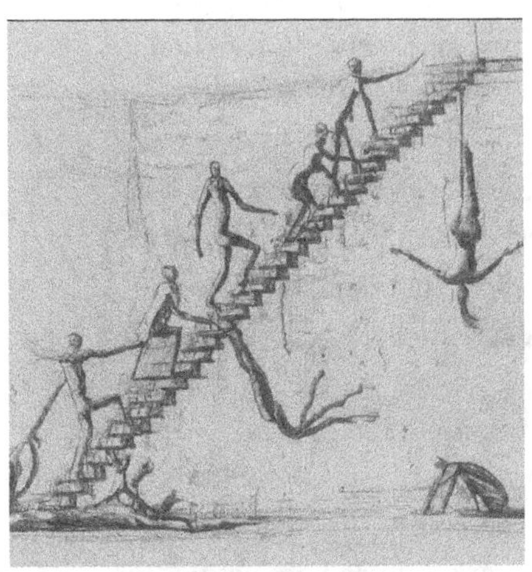

In the dance of life, two partners sway,
Success and failure, night and day.
One brings smiles, the other sighs,
Both are seen through different eyes.

Success a golden crown, a difficult peak,
Shines bright with joy, a triumph we seek.
Close behind a shadow creeps,
In absolute silence failure sleeps.

Yet are they not, these two we see -
The true sides of life's duality?
Success, the song a victor sings,
Failure whispers, wisdom it brings.

Success may crown our fleeting days,
With accolades and endless praise.
Yet failure moulds the life with care,
And builds a strength beyond compare.

So cherish both the highs and lows,
In every lesson that life bestows.
For in the depth that shadows lie,
Resilience grows, and spirits fly.

In the climb and in the fall,
We learn, we rise, we conquer all.
For in the end we come to see,
Success and failure both set us free.

Abandoned Memories

Standing silent, a forgotten shell,
Stories are whispered which walls now tell.
Empty eyes, staring back at the world
Tears dried up, nothing unfurled.

Faces blurred a fleeting scene,
A haunting echo, what could have been.
Echoes of laughter, a life once bright,
Now swallowed by shadow and fading light.

Like faded photos in a dusty frame,
A glimpse of joy, a whispered name.
A monument of dreams left behind,
A canvas of memories etched in mind.

Time a healer, mends a tear,
Leaving no bruise, everything clear.
Hope remains a flickering spark,
To piece together all the pieces scattered in the
dark.

A yearning deep, a silent plea,
Grasp the fragments, set the spirit free.
In the depths, where shadows hide,
Truth may slumber waiting to confide.

Caught in a downpour

The heavens weep, and let harmony descend,
A cleansing rhythm, that seems to never end.
Each drop like a note, a single beat,
On the thirsty earth, a welcome treat.

I step outside, to soak and breathe fresh air,
Saw the world unveiled, raw and bare.
No shelter sought, no need to hide.
Skin and soul soaked in the tide.

The drumming rain, it's a primitive call,
A cleansing fire, engulfing us all.
Distractions away, a mind set free,
In this downpour what do I see?

A glimpse of nature's might,
A humbling force, fierce and bright.
A reminder too, of life's fleeting flow,
Each drop a moment, to come and go.

Soaked to the bone and strangely whole,
I seek within, to see life's goal.
The rain persists, now a lullaby,
Reminding me of impermanence -
and my foolishness to reach for the sky.

Jog falls: A cascade of quartets

Western ghats in grandeur rise,
Jog Falls - a plunge, a misty surprise.

Raja, the King, a curtain grand,
Thundering torrent, hitting the land.
He plunges unbroken, a majestic way,
Stealing the breath in a watery spray.

Rani, the Queen - Oh! So serene,
Gliding down the cliff, a graceful queen.
Her silken veil shimmering in windy embrace,
A gentle cascade, a feminine grace.

Rocket - a furious, rapid descent,
A jet which is heaven sent.
He leaps in joyous display,
A dance of water, a playful ballet.

Roarer the name suggests, a thunderous call,
A roaring descent, conquering all.
His voice fills the air, a powerful resonance
A symphony of sound, a mighty presence.

Four falls united, a beautiful display,
Jog's vibrant drapery, steals heart away.
A timeless beauty, stays in memory's fold,
A cascade of quartets, a story to be told.

Embers of Breath

I watch every second scroll by to meet its minute
Every minute pining to complete the hour,
And every hour accumulating into years;
leaving visible lines on my face.
These I cherish.
'cause they make me who I am.

Then,
an awareness of a few more to come,
to carve, sketch and sculpt-
A portrait? A sculpture!

The one with an epitaph
....Life goes on...

Infinite Reflections

In every detail, a new world revealed,
Observation, a silent art concealed.
A careful gaze, a patient mind,
In quiet observation, many truths we find.

To witness beauty in every hue,
And uncover secrets, hidden from view.
With open eyes and a curious mind,
Details emerge of every kind.

Human interactions a complex play,
In every gesture, words convey.
Observing the rhythms of speech and tone,
Silence between the meaning is shown.

Slow your pace and truly see,
The world is a book, waiting for thee.
For in these quiet moments we find,
A deeper understanding of all mankind.

Family - Bond of Love

A woven thread, making the carpet grand,
Family's love binds one across sea and land.

Mother is the strength and a sheltering branch,
A source of wisdom and comfort during
emotional avalanche.

Father, silent guiding light,
In the darkest of hours shining bright.

Sister's laughter, a joyful sound,
Secrets whispered, hearts together bound.

Brother's loyalty ever so true,
A shoulder strong, to lean onto.

Children's giggles, like the sun rays
Chase the shadows and brighten the day.

Grandparent's stories, a treasure trove,
Seeds of wisdom from days of yore.

Age-old threads, unseen yet strong,
Keeping us on track, guiding us along.

Spouses our partners, hand in hand,
Life's ups and downs come always unplanned.

Through laughs and cries and life's rough tides,
We walk together, each to other a steady guide.

Cousins are friends, our hearts entwined,
We have shared memories and a playful bind.

Aunts and uncles, with open arms,
Offering us shelter from unseen harm.

Though threads may fray and colours fade,
The love that binds us, shall never be swayed.

It is a patchwork quilt, a vibrant scene,
Each piece a life, so serene.

A carpet woven, it is a gentle hold,
Family a story slow to unfold.
And in the long run more to be told.

The Half open door

In twilights gentle hue,
A hesitant life begins to stir.

Steps unsteady, paths unclear,
Wading through a veil of fear.
Opportunities beckon, whispers in the breeze,
But a wall of 'what if's' rises and actions cease.

Choices flicker, faint and shy
In the realm where doubts reside.

But within the hesitation, a flicker of something bold,
A yearning to break the silence and a story yet to be told.

Through the murmur of the heart,
Comes the strength to slowly start.

For even a life half lived, holds the chance to glow anew
To push past boundaries and chase the morning dew.

So embrace the timid stride,
In the hesitant do confide.
For within each faltering breath,
Lies the promise of whatever is left.

In the dusk light persists,
In every pause a chance exists.
Hesitant life though slow in pace
Carries a wisdom in its embrace.

Unclenching the fist

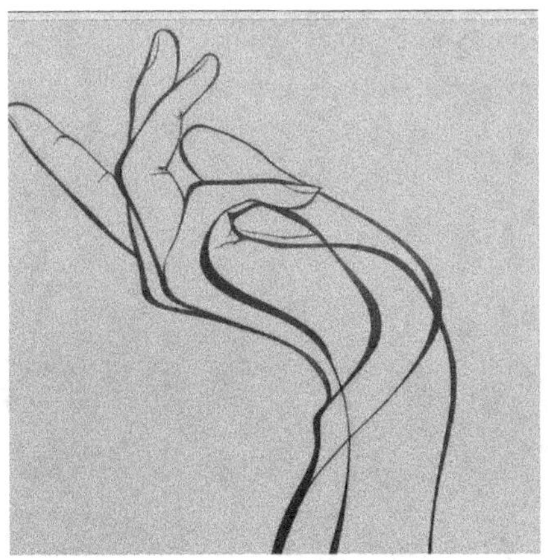

To let go is to breathe a sigh so deep,
To free the heart and mind from what we keep.
Casting off the burdens from the past,
Finding peace and healing that will last.

Saying farewell to old worn out pain,
Finding joy and to fill the space again.
Trusting the flow of light to guide,
Releasing fear and doubt we hold inside.

Let's feel the gentle breeze,
Welcome change, find new ways to ease.
Rising above the storm,
Embracing life in every form.

Letting go is a bittersweet embrace,
A scar heals, leaving a gentle space.
Life unfolds at a steady pace,
One finds solace in its grace.

Friendship with a Heartbeat

Love is fine bright and bold,
A warmth that chases away winter's cold.
Friendship blooms like a steadfast vine,
Bonding hearts in trust divine.

It's a hand with steady light,
Guiding through the darkest night.
Fanning the flame - a gentle breeze,
Strengthens love and sets it free.

Through laughters and through tears,
Friendship strengthens us & calms our fears.
Broad shoulders, a listening ear,
A bond that grows with every passing year.

When trials come and shadows fall,
Friendship's voice answers the call.
An understanding that's warm and true,
It bridges the gap between the two.

In every relationship we see,
Friendship's role is the key.
A love that is built on trust and care,
Endures thru' all that we bear.

Love and friendship forever bind,
Dancing together - flames entwined.
It's in their union we see,
The hope for all humanity.

Eternal Embrace

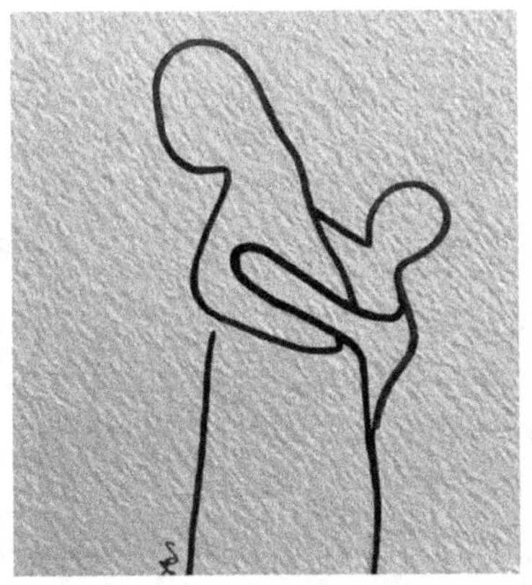

From tiny hands, to when dreams take flight,
Parents' love a constant light.
Through the first stumbles and scraped-up
knees,
Their gentle touch, brings complete ease.

When tears well up & shadows creep,
Their warm embrace is where worries sleep.
They whisper tales of strength and grace,
And plant a seed of hope to embrace.

No task too great, no load too small,
In their hug, we have it all.
A shelter in life's stormy weather,
A bond that fate has brought together.

Their sacrifices - unseen and vast,
They assist build our future and help face our
past.
With patience wisdom and endless care,
They teach us how to love and share.

Success we chase and our dreams take flight,
Their pride shines bright, always a guiding light.
Through choices made and paths unknown,
Their love remains a lifelong loan.

For though we grow and hearts may stray,
Parents' love will always stay.
A constant force unwavering and true,
Their actions whisper -"I'll always love you".

Innocence of a child

The world in the eyes of child is bright,
Every morning bringing new light.
Every laugh is pure and sweet,
In every puddle, joy they seek.

Giggles echo in the afternoon sun,
Endless things to do, always on the run.
Castles of sand reach up to the sky,
Rainbows whisper as they float by.

Hands are tiny, hearts are vast,
Trust is given really fast.
They see the world clear and bright,
Find the wonder in each and every sight.

Their dreams are a land of joy and play,
All sorrows tiny and kept at bay.
Let's keep their innocence close and near,
For in their world there is nothing to fear.

The becoming

In the womb of the earth, a seed lies,
Dreaming of reaching the open skies.
A tiny kernel brown,
Silent in the fertile ground.

Sunlight calls with a gentle touch
Rain caresses not too much.
Roots awaken, stretching deep,
In the earth is where they were asleep.

Tender sprouts with emerald hue,
Breaks the surface to feel the dew.
Leaves unfurl to greet the dawn,
The journey of life has just begun.

Seasons pass and years unfold,
Sapling grows both strong and bold.
Shade it gives - a heaven so sweet,
Shelter for the summer's heat.

Majestic oak, or weeping willow,
Stands tall creating a great shadow.
Each began a humble seed,
Now a mighty noble breed.

In every leaf and bark we see,
A tale of transformation free.
From silent seed to towering tree,
A timeless tale of mystery.

Pain of growth

Through every tear and every fall,
Learn to rise, and stand tall.
The pain of growth a bitter friend,
With every wound, a chance to mend.

The path we walk, so rough and steep,
Dreams haunt - troubled sleep.
Our hearts break and spirits mend,
We find strength and fears we fend.

In silent moments deep and still,
We feel a shift, a restless will.
A whisper in the heart, a call,
To rise to change, to face it all.

In our hearts the seeds are sown,
Through pain through tears we have grown.
With open arms we face the sun,
Embrace the journey, never done.

Weaving tales with threads of gold,
Strength deepens, a story unfolds.
In the end the truth is clear,
The pain of growth we hold dear.

Harmonious Cuisine

In a kitchen, bright with morning light,
Where pots and pans sing day and night.
The art of cooking pure and clean
With colours vibrant, fresh and green.
A choice of spices fragrant and bold,
Tell us stories ancient and old.

Cumin, turmeric and coriander's grace,
Together they form a warm embrace.
Tomatoes so ripe, with all they blend,
Creating a symphony that knows no end.

Chickpeas and lentils, humble and kind,
Millets offer sustenance to body and mind.
Caressed by Spinach, Kale and Chard
Each bite a blessing, taste buds on guard.

Rice a soft bed for curry to rest,
Broccoli, Cauliflower florets, they are the best.
A sprinkle of seeds - nuts, a dash of lime,
Transcends the mundane, turns every meal into a
fine dine.

From tuvar, moong, masoor dal, to hearty
paneer,

Each dish crafted with love and cheer.
A tribute to Mother Earth in every creation,
The art of cooking a celebration.

Let's gather both friends and kin,
In the kitchen is where we begin.
To honour mother nature's kind hand,
In every dish a story grand.

Silent speech of lines

In silence a world takes form,
From the murmurs of graphite soft and warm.
A blank canvas pure and white,
Awaits the dance of shadow and light.

In an artist's hand no move is wrong,
Each line a journey, each stroke a song.
The soul's reflection is quietly seen,
In gentle curves and edges keen.

Capturing the essence of each face,
Contours appear with flowing grace.
Every sketch a story's start,
Drawn from the depth of the heart.

An art that speaks without a voice,
A silent song of choice.
In every curve and shaded hue,
The artist's world comes into view.

In every sketch a glimpse of light
A testament of passion's might.
When dreams and reality come face to face,
A fleeting moment, a timeless space.

White rose path

Along the pavement, white roses bloom,
Soft whispers and disappearing gloom.

A pathway lined with nature's grace,
Each bloom like a gentle face.
Soft and gentle they unfold,
A beautiful white story to be told.

Like the face of the moon serene and bright,
Gleaming faces in the night.
A stroll in this lane,
Eases sorrows soothes pain.

White rose path, the name sounds sweet,
Where heaven and earth would love to meet.
In this beauty let's find peace,
Where all chaos briefly cease.